For Val

DEREK

For Steven & Jonathan

JOHN

Library of Congress Cataloging in Publication Data
Hall, Derek, 1930-   Otter swims. (Growing up)
Summary: With his mother's help, a young otter overcomes his fear of
the water and discovers the pleasures of swimming.
1. Otters—Juvenile literature.   2. Animals, Infancy of—Juvenile
literature.   [1. Otters]   I. Butler, John, 1952-   , ill.   II. Title.
III. Series: Growing up (Alfred A. Knopf)
QL737.C25H34   1984   599.74'447   83-22004
ISBN 0-394-86503-0   ISBN 0-394-96503-5 (lib. bdg.)

Otter Swims

By Derek Hall

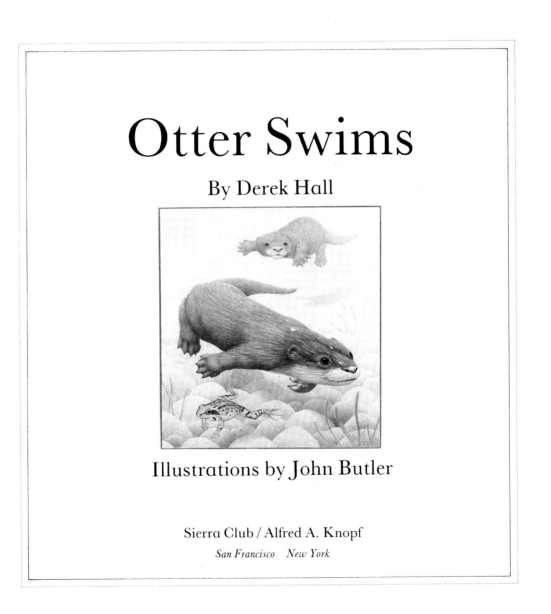

Illustrations by John Butler

Sierra Club / Alfred A. Knopf

San Francisco   New York

Otter's mother slides down a grassy bank and dives into the river. She does it again and again. But Otter only watches. He is frightened of the water.

This time she does not come back. Otter scrambles up the bank and stands on his hind legs to look for her. All he can see is a line of bubbles.

Otter bobs up and down
anxiously, staring hard at
the water. Suddenly he slips,
loses his balance, and topples
head over paws into
the river.

Otter panics. He tries to run through the water back to the bank. He paddles his legs up and down very fast and cries. His mother swims toward him.

Now Otter is not so
frightened. He swishes his
tail from side to side like
his mother. He's swimming!
He twists and turns and
glides through the water.

Otter feels excited. He takes a deep breath and dives down to explore. He sees fish flashing to and fro in the water and tries to catch one to eat.

When he gets out of the
water, Otter's soft, silky
fur is spiky and doesn't feel
right. But Mother shows him
how to dry himself as she
rolls and wriggles about
in the grass.

No sooner is he dry than
he wants to swim again.
Now Otter slides down the
slippery slope into the river.
Splash! It's lovely to play
in the water with Mother.